MW01119754

HOW DID THAT GET TO MY TABLE?
SALAD

BY EMILY J. DOLBEAR

COMMUNITY • CONNECTIONS
?

CHERRY LAKE
Publishing

Published in the United States of America by Cherry Lake Publishing
Ann Arbor, Michigan
www.cherrylakepublishing.com

Content Adviser: Anuradha Prakash, PhD, Professor, Food Science, Chapman University
Reading Adviser: Cecilia Minden-Cupp, PhD, Literacy Consultant

Photo Credits: Cover and page 1, ©miskolin, used under license from Shutterstock, Inc.; page 5,
©Dusaleev Viatcheslav, used under license from Shutterstock, Inc.; page 7, ©Tree of Life, used
under license from Shutterstock, Inc.; page 9, ©Jim West/Alamy; page 11, ©Mark Gibson/Alamy;
page 13, ©Jennifer Brown/Alamy; page 15, ©The Photolibrary Wales/Alamy; page 17, ©Blend
Images/Alamy; page 19, ©MBI/Alamy; page 21, ©allOver photography/Alamy

LIBRARY OF CONGRESS CATALOGING-IN-PUBLICATION DATA
Dolbear, Emily J.
  How did that get to my table? Salad / by Emily J. Dolbear.
    p. cm.—(Community connections)
  Includes index.
  ISBN-13: 978-1-60279-473-3
  ISBN-10: 1-60279-473-1
  1. Salads—Juvenile literature. 2. Salad vegetables—Juvenile literature.
I. Title. II. Title: Salad. III. Series.
  TX807.D65 2009
  641.8'3—dc22   2008047268

Cherry Lake Publishing would like to acknowledge the
work of The Partnership for 21st Century Skills. Please
visit *www.21stcenturyskills.org* for more information.

CONTENTS

DO YOU LIKE SALAD?

What's that pile of green stuff on your dinner plate? It's a **salad**! The most common kind is a garden salad. It might have lettuce, tomatoes, and carrots. Maybe you topped it with dressing. Do you like salad? Do you know where it comes from?

4

How many different vegetables do you see in this salad?

FIELDS AND GREENHOUSES

The vegetables we eat in salads grow on plants. The plants grow in fields and greenhouses. A greenhouse is a building made of glass or plastic. It has the right temperature and light for growing plants. Plants also need the right amount of water.

These tomatoes are growing in a greenhouse.

Vegetables need water, sunshine, and healthy soil to grow. Then it's time to gather the crops.

Lettuce heads and tomatoes are cut from the plants. Tomatoes are picked when they are still a bit green. They will ripen on their way to market. Carrots grow beneath the soil. Machines lift carrots from the ground.

Workers use machines to help them pick lettuce.

THINK!

Lettuce and carrots grow better in cooler weather. They are called cool-season crops. Tomatoes grow better in warmer weather. What do you think tomatoes and other crops that grow better in warm weather are called?

9

HEADING TO THE MARKET

What happens to the vegetables before they get to the store? Workers at **packing houses** wash the vegetables. That helps remove **germs**. Germs can make you sick. Machines spin the washed lettuce to dry it.

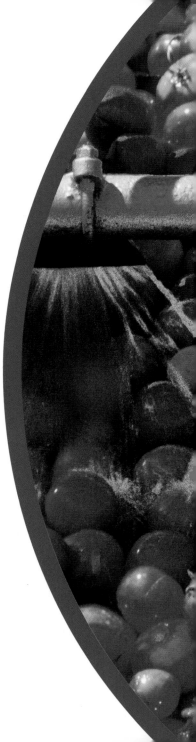

Machines wash the vegetables to remove dirt and germs.

Machines at the packing house wrap the washed heads of lettuce in plastic. Other machines pack washed lettuce leaves and carrots into special bags. The bags help keep the food fresh. Tomatoes usually go into plastic boxes.

Machines stamp a date on every package. The date tells how long you can store the food before it spoils.

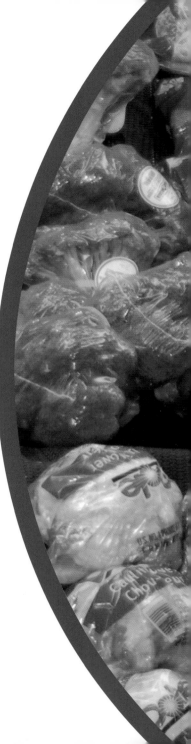

Many stores sell vegetables packed in plastic bags.

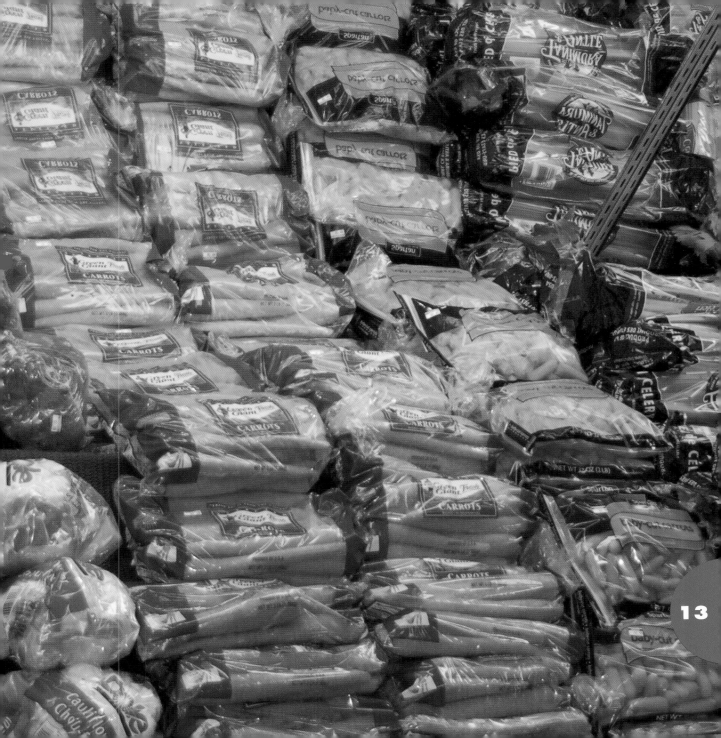

13

Then the vegetables are loaded onto cooling trucks. Vegetables must be kept cool to stay fresh. The trucks carry the vegetables to stores.

Trucks can carry many kinds of vegetables.

Look at the vegetables in the **produce** section. See if any packages have stickers showing where the vegetables were grown. Were any of them grown in another country? If they were, they probably came by airplane.

Workers at the store unpack the vegetables. They put them in the produce section. They are kept cool. Some vegetables also need to be kept moist. They are **misted** with a fine spray of water. This helps keep the vegetables fresh.

Store workers put vegetables in the produce section.

Lettuce leaves hold a lot of water. Do you think lettuce has **vitamins** in it? Make a guess. Check on a lettuce food label. Was your guess correct?

17

MAKE YOUR SALAD!

Now the vegetables are ready
to buy. Look for the freshest
vegetables. You want crispy,
green lettuce. Look for deep
red tomatoes. Pick out bright
orange carrots. Stay away
from vegetables with limp
leaves. Pass up vegetables
with rotting spots.

The freshest vegetables make the best salads.

The lettuce, carrots, and tomatoes you picked will make a tasty salad. Their trip from the farm to your table was a long one. The trip from the table to your mouth is a short one. Grab your fork and dig in!

Now you know where your salad came from.

Draw a picture of how salad gets from a farm to your table. Show all of the stops along the way. Share your drawing with a friend. Pictures help people learn new things.

GLOSSARY

germs (JURMZ) very small living things that can make people sick

misted (MIST-ed) sprayed with tiny drops of water

packing houses (PAK-ing HOUS-sez) buildings with equipment used to prepare and package vegetables

produce (PROH-dooss) fruits and vegetables that are grown for eating

salad (SAL-uhd) a dish of raw vegetables usually served with a dressing, sometimes made with fruit or other food

temperature (TEM-pur-uh-chur) a measurement of how hot or cold something is

vitamins (VYE-tuh-minz) substances in food that help people stay healthy

FIND OUT MORE

BOOKS

Graimes, Nicola. *Kids' Fun & Healthy Cookbook*. New York: DK, 2007.

Katzen, Mollie. *Salad People and More Real Recipes: A New Cookbook for Preschoolers and Up*. Berkeley, CA: Tricycle Press, 2005.

Leavitt, Amie Jane. *A Backyard Vegetable Garden for Kids*. Hockessin, DE: Mitchell Lane Publishers, 2008.

WEB SITES

Agriculture in the Classroom
www.agclassroom.org/kids/index.htm
Take a farm-related quiz, get some ideas for science projects, and take a virtual tour on a real family farm

Fresh for Kids
www.freshforkids.com.au/index.html
Click on the Fruit & Veg tab for a lot of information about fresh fruits and vegetables

INDEX

24

ABOUT THE AUTHOR

Emily J. Dolbear
works as a freelance
editor and writer
of children's books.
She lives with her
family in Brookline,
Massachusetts. Her
sons are learning
the joys of eating
delicious salads.